Wednesday's Child

Rhea Côté Robbins

Maine Chapbook Award

Rheta Press
Brewer, Maine

First Edition, 1997
First Edition, Second Printing, 1998
Second Edition, 1999
Second Edition, Second Printing, 2001
Second Edition, Third Printing, 2008

Published in the United States of America
by
Rheta Press
Brewer, Maine

Reprinted by special arrangement with
Maine Writers & Publishers Alliance

This book is printed on recycled paper

ISBN: 0-9668536-4-4
Library of Congress Catalog Card Number: 98-92339

"On the Road Between" was previously published in
The Puckerbrush Review XIV,i - Summer-Fall, 1995

"Something That Will Cure" was previously published in *L'Ouest
Français et la Francophonie Nord-Américaine, "De l'Ile à la
Tortue, à la Nouvelle France, à la Nouvelle-Angleterre: lutte
pour une identité vivable," Presses de L'Université d'Angers,
Angers, France, 1996*

Cover photo and
Pen and ink illustration by Rhea Côté Robbins

For my husband, David, his devotion to me and his support of my work—I am always happy to have his presence at my side and for all my children, my compass.

This work is in memory of my maman and dad, Rita St. Germain Côté and G. Raymond Côté, Sr.

Contents

Introduction

This is a book about a female growing up, living in, trying to leave her cultural self behind, and then returning to the Franco-American cultural group which exists in the Northeast, and more specifically in Waterville, Maine. The book addresses what has been asked of me in order to be present to this cultural group of people. As a girl/woman who or how have I been asked to be? What has been asked of me? The book is written from the perspective of a contemporary woman who is also an historical person. The book is also as much about the conditions in which the Franco-American group exists as well as the writing about what it means to be Franco-American and female. This is a book about how we are our historical self while we are in the present. I am more of my past—than I am of the present moment—when it is in the present moment that I now exist. What is, or is not, reflected in my reality and the reality of other Franco-Americans? This book is about the female self and her formation through the many individuals and institutions around her. Through story and cultural filters, the book illustrates family, friends, religion, health, alcoholism, superstitions, art & craft, beliefs, values, song, recipe, story, coming-of-age, generations, motherhood, language, bilingualism, denials, sexuality and what constitutes a cultural individual in a society that will not always allow that person full access or realization to who she is. But she does it anyway.

—*Rhea Cote Robbins*

Wednesday's Child

Monday's child is fair of face,
Tuesday's child is full of grace,
Wednesday's child is full of woe,
Thursday's child has far to go,
Friday's child is loving and giving,
Saturday's child works hard for a living,
And the child that is born on the Sabbath day
Is bonny and blithe, and good and gay.

The Family Treasury of Children's Stories—BOOK ONE
To my Godchild From your Godfather, May 26, 1959

"What A Clever Frenchwoman Says of Americans.—A good many Americans will remember *Madame Olympe Audanarde*, a French woman who sought among us fame and fortune as a lecturer. When home she published a book about us called "Le Far West," in which she says: "If not a 'Yankee' by birth or inclination, you will, after a residence of a few months in America, become a victim of a violent spleen—a strange inexpressible discouragement. The word 'business' is forever sounded in your ears, until a great longing takes possession of you to fly far out of this prosaic atmosphere."

She complains of the absence of filial love and genuine family life, but acknowledges that she is lost in admiring wonder at the process of national assimilation which is all the while going on— the annual recasting and fusion of 300,000 or 500,000 emigrants, mostly farmers; mechanics, and adventurers into one free enlightened and powerful people…"

—*The Waterville Mail, Vol. XXIV, No. 19, November 4, 1870*

If Not a Yankee By Birth

We can hold memory—precious or terrifying—a long time in us as a companion with whom we often hold counsel. Discuss the earlier uprooting as a recent event. Examine the tints, the shades. Echoes of the players loom out in brevity and bluntness.

I sit with my morning coffee, alone, the boys are gone to deliver the morning papers in the neighborhood, everyone else is asleep or reading, the memory jabs me. Am I allowed to begin again? Over and over, till I get the pieces in place? The past bellows, loud, and blows air on the flames of being. The heat presses on me like the hot bed of coals—long seasoned. Being French, Franco-American in Maine.

I am waiting days for the results from the biopsy. Patiently, or at least knowing I am separated from the lump. It is my eighth biopsy. With two bouts of cancer under my belt, breast cancer, radiation, heartache, doubt assuages, along with reconstruction of my sense of self, I feel lucky to be sitting here.

I am five years old begging the sixteen-year-old boys, one my brother, the others his friends, for a drink. After the operation and the ether, I am thirsty. I am in a hospital ward. A porch. Another brother is not far from me because we went into the hospital together, he and I, both of us are in the hospital to have our tonsils out. Bob and I. Twins of a sort. Both of us born in the month of May.

Born of a mother who is a twin. Rita of the Rita and Rhea twins. The *St. Germain* twins from Wallagrass. *Rita* is *ReeTah* when pronounced in French. *Maman* was ReeTAH!

I get my drink because I beg real good. I throw up soon after that.

"We told you. You should not have drunk the water."

My throat is dry and it hurts. The pain passes and somehow we get to eat vanilla ice cream. I embarrass my brother, Bob. Sometimes because I want to torment him in public and other times I am surprised at his anger at me because when no one is looking he is nice to me, but just as soon as people are around he is gruff again. He begrudges me his attentions. So I am in an emotional slingshot. I think I can control the temperature of his benevolence.

"Bob, my throat hurts."

"Shut up, you cry baby," he replies from his status of nine years old.

"How did you get the ice cream?"

"Ask for it." he commands.

Being older, he always had a better grip on the world around us. He took great pains and pleasure in flaunting his superiority.

When we were older and when I had my cancer, his cancer was much more serious than mine. Of course. I was only having radiation. He had to have radiation and chemo.

"Yours is just a baby cancer," he teased me. He knew how to keep my face off the floor. One challenge from him meant I could not let him win or show me up. It was all he had to say. Some things never change; I was thirty-two and he was thirty-six.

My newspaper delivery boys are back.

"Hurry up in that shower," the older one says.

"Why do I always have to hurry up for him?" my youngest asks. "Maybe I'll just have to lock myself into the bathroom and stay there forever."

Maybe I'll join you I think to myself.

I no longer slept in a crib, but when I went in for a hernia operation at age three they put me in a crib that resembled a cage. A stainless steel cage. I remember arguing with the nurse, *maman,* and being hurt in my baby pride that I was a big girl who had a big bed at home and now, at the hospital, had to sleep in a crib. I

16

remember distinctly the indignity I felt. All memories darken like old photographs. The walls are green and someone has turned down the lights. There's a dimmer switch somewhere in my mind.

My hospital roommate received presents. I did not. Not at first, and not as many as I would have liked. I wanted everything the other little girl had and I complained. Her *maman* stayed overnight with her. Mine went home. And I was left alone. *Maman* told me I was a "big girl" at age two or three. Even then I was supposed to prove myself and "be tough." Not like the rest of the world which was soft. I remember being in that crib and the feeling of being alone. I remember them telling me I would be all right. I remember being mad. I remember being taken out of the crib. And the relief.

At five, I was back in the hospital for a double hernia operation. Two on each side of my groin. I feel a pain in me, standing there in the hospital lobby, at the tops of my legs, just on the inside curve, in ghost-like quality, which never quite goes away. I am forever standing there wanting to sit down.

I recall the incident so well because it is the time and place where my conscious knowing began. It is the exact pinpoint of time when I woke from a deep, sheltering somnolence; the altered state of innocence in childhood came to a halt that day. I remember it well because I felt the door shut on my childhood self and I felt my apprenticeship into the female begin. My apprenticeship to adulthood began that day. (The wound of being French *avec les améritchains* all around you—being tough in *Franglais*—speech and body language dead giveaways.)

I was discharged from the hospital. My *maman* and dad came to get me and they were arguing in the hospital lobby. Apparently they always argued, but this time it was different because I knew they were arguing. In public. I was anxious to get them home and out of sight of everyone. I was anxious to be out of there.

Arguing in French. Short, clipped insults hurtling around our

17

heads like mortars. Crashing on the shiny, sterile hospital lobby tiles. They didn't seem to care or even know that I was standing there in acute pain. The argument was the more pressing matter. My pleas for them to realize the pain fell on them as an extra, added burden. An aside. My hernia operation's aftereffects were my only weapon to break through to their consciousness. That was when I began to speak in code. That was the time of my knowing.

"The first span of the Waterville and Winslow bridge is engaged in the raising process to-day. The others will be coming along in quick succession—if the river behaves."
—The Waterville Mail, Vol. XXIV, No. 8, August 19, 1870

If The River Behaves

Dreams can be so real that they are more than filaments of us. Stray and striated. I dream a life of exchanges—real and unreal, good and questionable, stark and sparse in its gifts. Gifts with lives of their own attached to them.

I wake to the physical reality of my *mémère*'s quilt. It is the second day of its official display in my bedroom on a makeshift quilt rack. I lie there and watch its pineapple pattern vibrate between the white and blue. I picture my *mémère* sewing the quilt at odd moments. Between birthing seventeen children. The quilt's sharp pointed edges converge, jig-jag.

Mémère created order out of chaos and placed the evidence in the cloth. A legacy of the women in our family. To take brokenness and make things whole again.

She was widowed during the depression with a family of eleven children under the age of fifteen. Her sewing needle fed her children. The quilt speaks of a leisure time which did not exist. How she managed to squeeze a quilt out of her life is miracle or miserableness made intangible. Or it could have simply been the work of habit. Hands never idle. The value of the quilt lies in its testimony to her determination of beauty measured by cloth.

I think how the quilt, which was promised to me—as my *maman*'s only daughter, came to be mine. In defense of myself against an army of family, I stand on the dignity of my only-daughter status, its legacy bearing power and that my *maman* told me I was to have the quilt.

Actually, there were two quilts I was to have. My *mémère*'s and my *maman*'s. We would sit on *maman*'s bed and talk about the squares in her quilt and what they meant to us. The quilt as a story board. My *mémère*'s quilt lay on a shelf in the closet in a heavy plastic bag. My *maman* never displayed her *maman*'s quilt because

20

she possessed it in the days before such things were valued as show pieces. Quilts were utility. The women's lives in our family were anything but show.

"When did *maman* die?" my brother asked.

"Almost two years ago," I reply. "In June. It has been almost two years."

All the family, my three brothers and me, the children of him and her, our parents, gather at the funeral home, along with our spouses. Our father, not quite two years after *maman*'s death, passed away that afternoon and we are there to pick his coffin and to make sure he is dressed well in death as he had been in life for other special occasions. The man had his pride. He would buy suits from the best stores in town. To let the world know this working man, this laborer, had good taste.

"When you buy something, always buy the best. It will last you," he often told me. It was advice his *papa* had given him. So he was buried in his best suit.

Somehow my brothers and their wives bestowed on me the task, as an honor, of going back into the house to get his clothes. I went alone.

The house had already become a place of ghosts, of haunts, of echoes. The house, hand built by my father and mother, had already acquired the feeling that someone was never coming back home.

The thought occurred to me to take the quilts, to take them on my first visit to get the clothes. I did not. I wanted the quilts— one my mother had made and the other one my *mémère* had made.

My *mémère*. A woman with seventeen children. One set of twins. One lost through the ice. One died due to accidental poisoning by her own hand in the middle of the night. One deaf because of spinal meningitis. And her quilt. Her quilt she made and ran out of fabric for a last square. She went down to the local

21

store, "*Grenier's,*" and purchased a piece to complete the final square. The quality of the fabric was not the same and so the one square yellowed over time and the rest of the white on the quilt remained white. She had given the quilt to her daughter, my *maman*, to fix the yellowed square. If anyone would fix it, *Rita* would. She was the one who had the determination to get the job done. She never did. And I never will. I like the oddness, the unevenness of the yellowed square.

I have had the quilts for eight years now, I think to myself. This is the first time I displayed *mèmère*'s quilt. Other children of my *mèmère* want the quilt. Or wanted it. My stealing something, which was already mine, given to me by my *maman* as the only daughter, put an end to questions about who would get the quilts—my *maman*'s and my *mèmère*'s. My self-vindication does not stop me from feeling guilty.

In my *mèmère*'s family of seventeen children I imagine that solid proofs of a mother's abiding love were scarce due to materialistic poverty. There were other kinds of proofs of love, but only one daughter received the quilt. For reason of repairs to be made. A reason which did not hold water.

There are taboos about stealing from the dead. It took me three tries to get the clothes right for my father to be buried in. I was thinking more of how I could take the quilts. I knew they would not be given to me, but to whoever else had requested them before me. The other relatives disapproved and said everyone should stay out of it and not ask for anything of my parents' estate. Extended family lines and loyalties are blurred at times like these.

I don't often choose clothes for the dead to be buried in. Once when my *maman* died and then, when my father died.

I chose socks with holes in them. Or his shirt was stained. On my third trip back into the house, alone, I took the quilts my *maman* promised me that I could have. I can lie well. I can look so

22

innocent and so pure because I don't often steal quilts from the dead. Only when I am desperate and I know someone else, someone from the other seventeen children of my *mémère* will want the prized pineapple quilt.

I was nervous about the theft of what was mine and I was giddy about what I had done. Thirty-one-year-old women don't usually go around stealing from the dead. Or the estate of the dead. Or the living relatives of the dead. Or the next of kin. Except I am all of those. The only female in a long line of strong men. It is difficult to be seen in that milieu. Probably, just as difficult to be seen in a family of seventeen. Fighting for space in a family is dirty business. One for which you hope the others can find forgiveness in their hearts.

I was a woman lonely for her *maman* and her *mémère* when I took those quilts. Mistakenly, at thirty-one, I was perceived as a little girl by my brothers who would never allow me my rightful place in the world of decision making. True, I was given the more homely tasks, but in decisions which involved the salt of life, truth and power, density of being, layers of presence, I was often made invisible and silent. I would not have been heard if I had only spoken my desire, or to remind my brothers what my mother had said to me about the quilts. I knew this and I had to act. At the moment it did not matter to me that I was one in a long line of many who wanted the quilts. The moment I took the quilts I became an individual in my own right. It was one time my place was not to be usurped by another. I would take my chances and I would risk shunning by the family for what I did.

Driving home, I told my husband, "They are in the back." I was sure what I had done showed on my face as I told him.

"What's in the back?" he asked.

"The quilts," I said looking guilty now that I was free from view.

"What quilts?" He looked at me seriously.

"I took the quilts. The ones *maman* said I could have."

23

I knew there would be some kind of hell to pay, but I did not care. It was the only way I could get them as I was meant to and I knew it. So much for unwritten promises *maman* made to me.

Strangely enough I got to keep the quilts and I'm not quite sure what everyone says about me behind my back, but I felt it was the adult thing to do so that my presence would be felt and real. I was always the youngest and the least heard. It's tough holding up the totem.

There is *mémère*'s quilt. On the rack. In my bedroom and it vibrates with a life much more intense than the patterns in the cloth. My *mémère*'s quilt. I am the daughter of a twin. My *mémère* had seventeen children. Those seventeen children all had children. I have the quilt.

"The Kennebec Baptist Association met at West Waterville last Tuesday afternoon and organized by the choice of Rev. C. Parker of Norridgewock as chairman and Rev. William Clark of Mt. Vernon as clerk...Interesting discussions were had upon various topics, during the three days session, and in response to urgent appeals it was decided to put a colporter into the field, and Rev. Mr. Burrage, Rev. Dr. Wilson and Mr. C. F. Hathaway, of Waterville, were appointed a committee to find the right man for the place and procure the funds for his support..."

—*The Waterville Mail, Vol. XXIV, No. 11, September 9, 1870*

Interesting Discussions Were Had
Upon Various Topics

A woman's life is full of interruptions. Broken moments and hours of servitude—voluntary and involuntary. The prayers of sainthood on our breaths or the curses of hell at the heels of what crashes a moment's peace or solitude. The day comes when the woman is faced with herself. She can find no other but her alone in this great big house. She has only to re-begin her life, now. Decide in her later years what it is she wants to do with what is left of her. Or a woman sits at her sewing machine and runs a few strips of cloth toward her independence on a regular daily basis. I am that woman and my *maman* was that woman as her *maman* was that woman.

My daughter is who she's going to be in this. She pieces cloth like the women who pieced cloth before her, and she pieces music like cloth, giving gifts of musical patchwork.

Other women I know run the cloth through the sewing machine, but it is their factory life's existence. My mother-in-law is one of these women. Thirty-three years of sewing one part or another of men's shirts. The high quality kind. Hathaway shirts at the C.F. Hathaway Shirt Factory on Water Street. Their ads show Grecian, fine-chiseled featured men with impeccable suits and baby-soft cured leather shoes and gloves. Camel's hair long coats. White silk neck scarves. The retirement check of this woman after giving a lifetime to the sewing mill is $137 a month, and after six months of retirement, she no longer qualifies for health insurance. She is forced to buy her own health insurance plan independently. The shirts sell for $50 to upwards of $70 apiece in the men's shops which sell quality clothing.

I was destined for the men's shirt factory mill. As so many of my neighbor women were destined.

I do not pride myself on the escape. I always meant to come back and tell you of the different kind of piecing my women, women of my French culture and women of other cultures, have had as a way of life. A serious way of life; an honorable employment. Hard-working people. *Ça travaillait forte c'monde là.*

I have heard stories all my life of these women in the shirt factory. A revolving door sort of place. A place where there are opportunities to go home and have a nervous breakdown, a baby, a change of heart and mind, only to come back later on when you can. A place which requires the women to buy their own scissors, an essential tool of the trade, like the master craftspersons they are. A shirt begins from the top of the building where it is cut and proceeds down through the floors, stops long enough at each block to have the whole-made-pieces, pieced to whole again, on to the basement for final inspection, packaging, and shipping. The building is brick-oven hot in the summer with women fainting from the heat, machine-warm in winter, sitting on the edge of the river which sometimes, in Spring, floods the parking lot. Work starts at 6:00 A.M. in summer to allow the women to leave early before the building heats up beyond human endurance. Or so that is how the process has evolved over the years. Voted in by the union.

Negotiating a day off is reason for a visit to the office and being made to cry by the boss. On the other hand, if on any given day there is not enough work for a worker to stay, then they are sent home without pay or apology. The hazards of the factory.

Recently the women punched out and were paid their averages in order to do inventory. A momentary pause or release from the mesmerization of the machines. To perform the yearly counting ritual. How are we doing? On a good day, an expert, old hand at this can sew up to 120 dozen. Which makes for good pay. Careful not to upset the bosses, mostly men. The women bring batch tickets home in their purses so their averages will remain average. The company figures that if you sew above your averages then the

27

job is too easy for you. If you get too good on a job, they'll move you to another job. One you have to learn how to do from the beginning. A self-destroying type of self-governance to keep your averages, average. You can't be too good on the job, or else.

Of course, bringing batch tickets home in your purse is not allowed. But they do it anyway. Living on the edge caught between performance levels of sewing too fast, too good and the fear of being fired. Breaking company unwritten and written policy. A woman apart from all the women, sewing on her collar stays, pockets, collars, cuffs, bands, shirt fronts and backs. Yes, women's lives are full of interruptions, but more importantly, a woman's life is knowing how to put those interruptions into a coherent whole.

"Every family needs to keep in the house something that will cure headache, toothache, ague pain, lameness, bruises, cramps and other kinds of pain and suffering, and what is there so good as Renne's Pain Killing Magic Oil. Try it. Sold by I. H. Low & Co."
—*The Waterville Mail, Vol. XXIV, No. 18, October 28, 1870*

Something That Will Cure

When I had cancer the second time, the time I lost my left breast, I lived far away from the shirt factory by then. I know women in my family who work there, but I had been gone from the sight of the mill, within walking distance from my home for many years. There are many women, maybe 500 or so who work in what I fondly call "her mill." There is the male equivalent in my hometown of "his mill." I often refer to "his and her mills" when I speak or think of my people. I had been gone from "her mill," and the women who work there are of my people—the French-speaking or French cultural people whose ancestors originated 400 years before from France.

Ironically, the Statue of Liberty, given to the United States from France as a gift symbolizing freedom was not necessarily meant for the French immigrants who came to the U.S. via the land bridge from Canada. For the French people immigrating to the U.S. in the 1600s, the statue should be relocated somewhere in the St. Lawrence. There the French would also need a translation of "give me your hungry and your poor..."

The women who work in the mill, and whose aspirations have much to do with the dominant society under which their ancestors came to rest and be employed by, still speak the language of their ancestors. Or if not, it is apparent in their demeanor, gesture, and their esprit de corps. Body language. It speaks to me. That and the magic the women weave over the years. The superstitions I grew up with. Holy Water sprinkled on the windows during a rainstorm to prevent the lightning from striking. Are we going to have a field day tomorrow? Put your Virgin Marys in your windows so we will have a sunny day. Talisman of luck; omens of fortune—good or bad—ran in close existence to reality. Hat on the bed, eating utensils falling on the floor, itchy noses, open umbrellas in the house, spilt salt and more. The secular were not as mystical or as powerful as the sacred keepers of ourselves, our children and our men. Scapulars were the death-defying cloth medals on string which could keep you from drowning in the mighty Kennebec, pour l'amour du bon Dieu.

I had been gone from the mill for many years when I had cancer the second time and I lost my left breast. News travels fast that travels unofficially. Among the women workers was a sacred woman; a holy woman. A woman of God. I never saw her face and she has never seen mine. She reaches across the distances I have traveled and she calls me to the banks of the river once again. Her hand reaches out to bring me home across a divide no mile could ever measure. She, in the language of my people, in our prayers, from my deepest memory, my oldest self—older than my lifetime—reaches out to me in my ordeal of breast cancer and sends me a scapular medal and murmurings in the French language prayers which can evoke providential personal assistance. Through the grapevine of women, this holy woman gave to my mother-in-law to give to me, her gift of scapular medal which I hung on my bedpost where it remains to this day. I have never set foot in the mill a moment of my life other than to shop in the "seconds" store, and it does not matter that I live far away in body, I can be recalled.

"'Roneka, The Forest Queen' is the title of an original operetta written by a young lady of this village, to be performed at Town Hall on Friday evening of next week. The parts will all be taken by young ladies—among whom will be musical talent that promises an attractive exhibition."

—*The Waterville Mail, Vol. XXIV, No. 20, November 11, 1870*

An Attractive Exhibition

Wednesday's children are those who are born in the middle of the week. Somewhere in the middle of it all. Wednesday's children get it from both ends. Sometimes it is something good and sometimes it is something not so good. They used to say Wednesday is Prince Spaghetti Day. That was for the Italians. There were not too many Italians in the town I grew up in. The French people ate spaghetti anyway. Too much, according to my older brother. He refuses to eat *"spaghet"* to this day. When I married I learned to make spaghetti so good, people told me I must have Italian somewhere in me. What I wanted to do, was to make an economical meal which reminded you of wealth. Of nights in Italy which came through the sauce. Sometimes, I'd bake an Italian bread, too. Mostly, I made white bread. Four loaves every week when I was first married. It would cost me ten cents a loaf to make. Friends would come over and hope it was bread baking day. You do something that often, for a long time, you get good at it and then the heart goes out of it and the skill goes somewhere back there in memory like a great being or presence it is. Some days, I let my bread baking come back to me. I wonder who I used to be and what I was like back then. Before I had my children, or before people died, or before I had cancer. Nobody who was close to me was dead yet. I think of the time when I began to sort things out for myself. Coming from where I came and going to where I am going.

I step away from my French beginning often. From my Franco-American neighborhood. I am on a search for a classical existence. One of white lights **only** on the Christmas tree. I arm myself to the teeth in hopes of leaving myself behind. The one who lives in a neighborhood of French speaking peoples.

Neighborhood as concrete sidewalks sloping sideways on the

way to school. Fighting who would walk next to whom. I was always fighting for the middle. The middle meant you could hear everything that was said and that you could be the one next to the popular girl, which was not the one in the middle, but the one on the end and the other girl on the other end had to be kept away from the popular girl.

We played a dodge game when we walked home. A fight for space or place where our importance in the social order fell in step with who walked closest to the popular girl. I was the highest in the social order because of how I figured out to walk in the middle. Until I told no one, my status walking home was quite high. I fought for the middle spot and we would walk home jostling each other to maintain the horizontal queen of the sidewalk. Popularity came to a person by a special benediction from God. No one needed to point out this special benediction from God because we could feel the dispensation in the girl. She had the longest, dirtiest finger nails on a little girl I had ever seen. Her nails shocked me, but her sense of person was so fine that we only mentioned the nails once amongst ourselves and that was years later when she had discovered the miracle of the fingernail file. My own nails were kept clipped short and bleeding at all times. I practiced several forms of cannibalism and self-destruction. I also ate my brown paper bag book cover off my books and the mohair yarn from Gabrielle's newly knitted beret. I gutted pencils and used their erasers as chewing gum. The nun would say, "Spit out the chewing gum. And stay after school tonight."

I'd spew chewed eraser into the trash and go home on time.

The ritual of biting my nails to the quick and all the skin surrounding the nails was a point of pride and a show of extreme I-don't-care. Biting the inside of my mouth seconded the air of nonchalance and furthermore ensured the middle ground I had acquired for myself on the sidewalk morning, noon and night. I maintained an aura of I am tough and don't you mess with me by

34

several female chest puffing rituals that I personally devised. Some were taken from my brothers and family habits which I adapted and implemented with huge success. In the land of parochial school in order to survive you had to have a gimmick. My way of rising above the Christian, Catholic crowd was to refuse to run in any popularity contest when I failed to break through "Red Rover, Red Rover send Rhea right over" and was laughed out of the game and when the cheese began to smell when we played "Farmer in the Dell."

"Farmer in the Hell," I think to myself now.

Compared to Catholic parochial school, my sandbox guy friends were nice. At least with them we could decide on a game or a way of being. Catholic school children playing Monday through Friday on the Sunday church parking lot, because the church was on the third floor over the school, develop a hardness of being which does not allow for a touch of the humane. We live a complicated system of reward and punishments. Reward is singular because that came only at the end of the year; punishments were daily. Mostly for who or what you were. Ethnic cleansing in the case of parochial school meant to dehumanize you to the point of prayer—to be re- leased from this private hell. So, in order to survive, you develop tactics which are not healthy. The abuse begun in the classroom, continued outside in the yard. Everything was divided according to sex—gender. Boys on one side; girls on the other. A crack in the sidewalk determines your sex. One step over the line while the patrolling nun's back was turned made you a hero or got you a punishment. We all knew we were sinning when we stepped over the crack to the boy's side, but we sinned anyway. If you were caught stepping over the line you got either a look of reprimand which you immediately mimicked when the nun's back was turned on her Angelus patrol or you had the opportunity to stand with your face pressed against brick for the rest of the recess.

One year, due to our continued unpious playing during the

ringing of the Angelus, the nuns came up with a idea. At the strike of noon when the church sexton faithfully rang the Angelus, we were to cease our pagan playing—stop all motion—and pray. A short prayer, mind you, but with a mindfulness to our dear God—*nôtre bon Dieu*. The message was delivered en masse to the entire school. Tomorrow when *M. Thibodeau* rings the bells, stop your playing, and pray. The nuns thought they had infiltrated the yard at last. Our indoctrination would be complete. The bells rang, the children stopped, but it is how we stopped that forced the nuns to rescind their request and to tell us to continue playing at the ringing of the Angelus.

As the bells rang, we froze in motion however we were. Our grotesqueries grew with each passing day. We devised a contest to see who could come up with the best deformed body pose to pray in. I often wonder at the tableau we presented to the surrounding apartment dwellers. At the stroke of noon the entire schoolyard of 300 or more children would deaden to a silence and freeze in motion as if time frozen. When the bells ceased their ringing, action would resume with the feeling we had never dropped a second. Crash the boy into the wall, jump the rope, tag the boy inches away just unthawed, twirl the girl, bounce the ball, roll the marble. The anticipation before the bells rang grew to a pitch and volume of scream, delight and decadence to match Mardi Gras. The nuns removed the request when they saw their only recourse was to jail us all. The Angelus rang over the heads of playing, running, jumping, screaming unhypocritical children for the rest of my stay at Notre Dame School. Give good Catholic children a religious artifact and we could undo its mystification or power in five minutes. We became expert at deflecting punishment.

Forced to eat the lunch? Throw it up. Go to confession too often? Make up some sins. Splash the holy water too fast with your fingers and before you know it the font is empty. In later years, go into the church during recess and light all the candles or blow them out depending on how you feel. All as a matter of sabotage and undoing the too strict ritual placed on ordinary children who were expected to be at all times—temples of God. Temples of Doom.

"Rum! Levi Lashus [*LaChance*], a Frenchman, who "keeps open quarters" in the old building next north of the Williams House, was investigated Wednesday morning by officer Edwards. Two packages or bottles of liquor were found—one in his boot and the other in a hole in the plastering. He was taken before Justice Drummond and fined $50 and costs. Lashus had just been legally warned out of the premises, on the supposition that he was selling liquor in violation of law—thus rendering the owner liable for heavy fine. Probably he will be expelled as soon as practicable, as the place has long been known as a bad one."

—The Waterville Mail, Vol. XXIV, No. 4, July 22, 1870

One In His Boot And The Other In A Hole

The tiniest elements remind me of the longest days. My life now, so far away in time and space, cannot be easily explained by what is physically around me. But I have become who I have become because of all those tiny elements coming into place one at a time. I look at people in a crowd and I think how each one of them got here. Some woman somewhere took the time to be pregnant so that another human being could come to life. Nine months of hostessing. And then if the cards are played right, eighteen to twenty years, no—a lifetime of mothering with a few breaks in between if you get lucky or a baby-sitter comes along.

But a certain smell, a certain look or dish. A fly on the wall. Wallpaper hangers and men on stilts swirling on a new ceiling with plaster after *mèmere* had died. Her house was filthy and we were fixing it up to rent. Her sons, two of them, both alcoholics, one smart; and the other retarded and reputed to be gay, sold their blood for beer money. The retarded one, he's kind of slow they told us kids, killed neighborhood cats for supper. Cat tastes just like rabbit they told me in reply to my disgust. What is he supposed to do? Starve? Cross-eyed, pigeon-toed, and a stutterer. *Mon oncle Pet. Mon oncle Pet-Pet* for short. Fart-Fart we used to call him behind his back. We didn't think it was a name that was bad. It was more a sound to go with the character of the man. One of the unfortunate ones. The neighborhood was full of them, so he wasn't that outstanding as far as characters go. Besides, he was just my uncle. A member of the family. We used to roll his and uncle Clem's cigarettes on Sunday afternoons when *mèmere* was still alive and the whole family would get together to drink beer, talk, smoke cigarettes and *lament*, as *maman* would say.

"Les moudgits lamenteux." maman would say. *"Moudgits làche. Ça sait pas faire rien. Et ses sœurs la même moudgits chose.*

39

Lamenteuses."

"I can't," she'd mimic wincingly. But then they would bring her new wool in the fall and it was *maman* who would sew my two cousins new winter coats. For awhile. Till *maman* put her foot down.

"They can sew their own goddamned coats," she said. Dad had really treated her bad that weekend. She wasn't about to eat his shit and theirs, too. "I am the smart one," she'd exclaim to his calling her *"moudgits dâsse"* all week-end. "Yeah, you're the stupid one," I would say under my breath to him echoing her.

Theirs was a double marriage in the families. An older sister of dad's and an older brother of *maman*'s had married earlier on. Family slung gossip said about the older couple that the husband was a drunk and the wife was reputed to be lazy. Depending from which family you were slinging the slander. The feud between the two families was well established long before *maman* and dad were married. So when dad brought *maman* home to meet his *maman* and *papa*, she was not well received. My father said too often to my mother that he married her out of revenge. So that she could pay for what her brother had done to his sister. That, in his more drunken moments, was his claim to why he married my mother. When he was sober he was more penitent and sorrowful as to what he had said and done. Come Monday morning before he went to the mill, it was her turn to talk. The woman was angry. And she slammed his lunch into his lunch basket for him to take to the mill and she crashed the cover down on his thermos full of coffee she had funneled in and she gave him a piece of her mind. "If you think..." They'd load up the cannon and start all over again come Friday night.

One time when we lived on the farm in Detroit, Maine *mon oncle Pet-Pet* came to help us on the chicken farm. He would be too drunk, blind from his crossed-eyes or *gauche* because, after he had been in the barn, we'd find dead chicks—the ones he had

40

stepped on. The work was too complicated for him.

But he was good at making us laugh. We could act silly with him.

"Say '*penut, penut, penut*' tree times widout laughing," he challenges us. Spitting and laughing, wiping his mouth free of backwash from the beer with the back of his shirt sleeve. He takes another a swig of beer. He has buck teeth, too. And he has a lisp. He is a clown with no need for a mask or makeup.

Dad didn't like us laughing at him.

"Say it! Quick. *Vite!* '*penut, penut, penut!*'" he giggled.

So we would try.

"*Penut, penut...*"

He sat, with his eyes bugged, his fly unzipped, holding his Schlitz by the neck, silently mouthing the words along with us.

My brother would crack up!

"I can't, *mon oncle*, I can't do it!" my brother would give up after three or four tries.

My turn. I would try.

"*Penut...*"

"ha...ha...ha...ha..." *mon oncle Pet* would snigger.

"*Mon oncle*, don't make me laugh."

"OK, OK."

"*Penut...*"

"ha...ha...ha...ha..."

"*MON ONCLE!*"

"OK, OK. I won't laugh," he'd say.

"*Penut...penut...*"

"ha...ha...ha...ha..."

"*Mon oncle*, you said you wouldn't laugh!"

"Did I? I won't laugh dis time. Just say it—tree times: '*penut, penut, penut.*' I bet you can't do it"

"Oh, yes, I can. See. '*penut, penut, ha, ha, penut.*'"

"Doesn't count," he said, "because you laughed."

41

"No, I didn't."

"Yes, you did. I heard you laugh." "See," he said, "you say *'penut, penut, penut'* tree times widout laughing."

"Let me try again!"

"OK. Dis is the last time."

"Penut, penut, penut," he says tree times. "No laughing. *Ris, pas!*"

I turn my back to him. *"Penut, penut, penut!"*

"T'as besoin de me garder, là! See, I told you you couldn't do it."

"Penut, penut, penut!" he crowed. And took another swig of beer.

"When the first French-speaking immigrants appeared in Waterville, this 'Plains' section of the town was a vast, thickly wooded area with a few tiny clearings here and there for grazing. The whole section up to what is commonly known as the 'flat' was a sort of peninsula, surrounded on the East side by the Kennebec River and on the West by a narrow, marshy stream having its source at the further end of Pine Grove Cemetery. This muddy brook slowly curved along today's King Street and emptied into the Kennebec Canal around the bottom of today's Sherwin Hill...

...Others found similar work in Waterville in the 1830's and 1840's. Some robust French Canadians were hired during that period to clear an extensive wooded area which was to become, in 1851, the Pine Grove Cemetery."

—Albert Fecteau, Master's Thesis, 1951
The French Canadian Community of Waterville, Maine

The Pine Grove Cemetery

All the vegetation around us has a way of knowing our secrets. The trees droop their leaves spying on our lives. The grasses bend their blades to catch our sounds. And then they gossip about what we have been up to lately. They know the pasts of whoever has been around. You can feel it in their eerie silence as they stand there or as you walk by. Whenever I face west, I face the setting sun, Garden of Eden's hidden gates and eavesdropping, chattering trees. Spreading rumor. Tattling. The trees and grasses know. It is their mystique. Their power. When I face west and I imagine I am seeing Garden of Eden, even as a child, I am seeing the gates to the Tree of Life. The trees are angels in disguise. The trees imitate Garden of Eden's special opening, and the younger you are the more magic you are, so you can see more of the underworld—the secret world all around us.

As a child I am in awe of the make believe because of the reality it carries. The possibility of chance. One of my walking home from school fantasies was that when I get home from school there will be a tractor trailer truck full of toys I won in a contest. I never entered my name, but someone did enter my name for me.

You hear about Charlie Verrow who dresses up in his Superman costume and jumps off the roof of the garage and breaks his arm and nose. Everyone wonders what got into that kid's head. Too much TV they say. I sit there wondering—what went wrong? He should have been able to make the leap. I shake my head like everyone else, copying them, but inside I think to myself, I bet I could do it.

What? Jump down all thirteen stairs in one jump and land on my feet at age four? Of course. I can do it. I do it all the time when I get tired of going down the stairs the regular way.

A hand reached out and grabbed us from that grave, I tell my friends years after the event happened.

I'm sure the man in a long duster raking leaves in the cemetery looked just like Michael the Archangel. He was standing guard, making sure we wouldn't get into Garden of Eden. After one of our raids, I saw him framed by an apocalyptic sky when he stood at the top of the hill, pointing at us with one arm to mark us as doomed. We locked ourselves in the shed, my brother, me and Jerry-Ron-and Ricky. Just in case.

Do the angels on the granite pedestals at the entrance of the cemetery blowing their horns, covered with gold leaf, come to life at the end of the world? I bet they do. I can almost hear them announcing the end of the world today. Every time we drove by on our way to Belgrade and Great Pond, my brother would point out the angels.

"Those angels are going to come alive at the end of the world," he says. We are sitting in the back seat of the Rambler.

I'm forty-one turning into the driveway to the Catholic side of the cemetery to go see my parents who are buried there and my brother who gave me those end of the world predictions for the angels coming back to life and I think about what he told me. I hope he's right.

My brother died when he was forty-one. You never think you are going to make it past the age of the person who died that you feel close to. He and I were always in the cemetery—playing. It was our playground when we were kids. To come see him buried here is one way of being magic. Our ghosts linger around the headstones. They keep burying new people here, but back then, when we were kids, we kept track of the new, fresh graves. Like we were the inspectors. Grave inspectors. Children loose in the graveyards—Protestant and Catholic—a fence divided those who were going to heaven and the eternally damned. To a Catholic, to be buried on the Protestant side was the same as going to hell and doomed. No

45

questions asked. Here was hell and here was heaven. Garden of Eden was at the bottom of the hill. Before you got to hell. Which was the Protestant side of the dead.

People would say to *maman*, "How can you live next to all those dead people?"

"It's not the dead that bother you," *maman* would say to shut them up.

In the woods, on the hill, playing as children, we came upon two graves: one was marked "Mother," and the other was marked, "Baby." The two markers, solitary in the brush, stopped us dead in our tracks. We ran home to tell dad and *maman*. They both knew the graves were there. The old cemetery had been on the side of the hill, he told us, and they decided to move the graves to the top of the hill. For some reason the city did not bother to take the mother and child. Why? How did she die? Was it in childbirth? No, I don't think so, *maman* said, because they would bury the baby with the mother then. Was she French like us? No, because the gravestone is old and it would have been written in French. Where did she come from? Probably somewhere in Waterville. Maybe she was a poor person, *maman* told me. Poor people were buried by the city in a pauper's graveyard. That was a city plot once. She probably was too poor to be buried anywhere else. Do you think there is a father buried somewhere near them? Maybe she had the child all by herself. Back then, that would have been a shameful thing to do. I don't know about her, you ask so many questions, talking machine. *Maman* was done talking about the woman and baby in the woods.

I went to visit the lone graves by myself. They were hard to find in the thick woods. Separated from the rest of the dead as if they were shunned in death as I imagined the mother and child had been shunned in life. I made up a life for the woman and her child in my mind. I clothed her. I gave her a house. I designed clothes for her baby. I let her live. I stood by them to talk and stare

46

at the headstones as if they would talk back and then I sat on the baby's headstone because it was small when I got tired of standing and talking to them. I would tell them everything was going to be O.K. I knew she was there. I knew she was dead. I knew she was all alone. I would not forget the Mother and Baby. No one remembered who she was. It didn't matter.

My grave plot is beside my brother's—my long-ago cemetery playmate.

As children we walk the roads in the cemetery. The place seems endless and far away from home. We drag sticks behind us. We have a special way of walking when we are in the cemetery. One for all seasons. In summer, we lope and drag sticks behind us leaving a trail like Hansel and Gretel to find our way back home. In fall, we pile the leaves and jump off the top of the hill down its slope. In winter, if you step lightly on the snow, you don't break through. Only the headstones are visible. We sit on the wrought iron lawn furniture in the winter breeze. Spring makes the whole road system muddy and the sap runs in the trees. We go every night to collect the sap from the line of maples running up the hill. There is a brook nearby. We have a meeting tree at the top of the hill. Every day at a certain time we meet there with the other neighborhood kids to decide who we have to scare first. Each other or the cemetery men. They are the workers who have parched brown skin, are silent like ghouls, smoke, and wear dusters. They scare us more than we know. But one of our favorite games is to try to sneak up on them, headstone-to-headstone, six or seven kids all at once and scream, ahhhh! at the cemetery men to see if we can get them to chase us. That's when we head for the shed.

So my brother is buried in our playground. The children playing with the dead. I like the bravery of the deed now. Back then, it was just a place for us to play. Ask the trees, they can tell you all about us.

"The migration of these sturdy French Canadian immigrants, often know as *'Canucks'* was very puzzling and sometimes annoying to some native citizens. Each year their number increased and the line of Yankees retreated...In the early days there was bitter feeling between the young men of the 'Plains' and the young men of the town...the struggle...stemmed from personal animosity and hatred...by the end of the 19th century, they had reached a point where their presence merited consideration."

—*Albert Fecteau, Master's Thesis, 1951*
The French Canadian Community of Waterville, Maine

Canucks

Spirits walk past us and leave their scent. It is the only way that the formerly alive can communicate with us—by leaving a smell behind. Or a blast of cool air. Like swimming in a spring-fed lake, every now and then you swim through a cool spot. Lying awake last night in my bed I smell something. It was a little unpleasant, but not entirely. Some spice. Crank shaft grease. Sawdust. Fish scales. Hot chili peppers. All mixed into one. Lying awake, unable to sleep all night, I knew my father was nearby.

Today is his birthday, I think to myself. If he were alive. Born at the turn of the century, his sensibilities were of a 19th century man. He was lost in the 20th century. I think he had lost his bearings when his father and grandfather entered the mill to work. *Pepère* worked at the Hollingsworth and Whitney and then tended his inner-city farm. My father was the good son who helped his *papa*, as he called him, with the farm animals, raising vegetables, and selling the produce to local people. They had corn on the cob for sale by July 4th. During the Depression they sold it to the rich people at a dollar a dozen. *Pepère* wore garters on his sleeves when he worked. He was a farmer by heart; a mill worker by fate. Too many mouths to feed in *Québec*. So *pepère's papa* walked from Canada to the U.S. and worked on farms to make his way. He came to Waterville. Married a local woman and settled in to the routine of turning a farmer into a city slicker.

Waterville, a township on the Maine map, is not a large land mass, but it is heady on its own fumes because of the Ivy League school which makes its home there—Colby College. The workplace for many Franco-Americans as cooks, janitors, secretaries and maids. Zamboni drivers. Toilet bowl cleaners. Salad preparers. Rarely do Franco-American children attend Colby College. Although children of workers can attend for free. Few choose to stoop to

49

that level of social climbing. Who would they talk to when they came back from the foreign land, and while there, who would understand them? The French body language is all different than what is bodily believed in at the Ivy League school. The gestures of being brought up French do not prepare a child to compete in the world of high finance, Jaguars, the smell of money emanating from the leather of the shoes and lying down in bed with creamy-skinned, silken-haired silver spun women. Or, men. So Colby is safely tucked away from the onslaught of the French who took up residence in Waterville to work in the mills. The women of my neighborhood were the playthings of the Colby men. "The girls on Water Street" were girls the Colby men were told to avoid. They might get the crabs. I am one of those women who the Colby men were told to avoid on a Saturday night. Their spirits stank when they walked in our neighborhood. It was the rotting shoe leather.

Pepère gambled. He gambled in the backroom of *Druoin's Cafe* with other men. During the Depression he amassed a sum of $10,000. Five card stud. As his granddaughter, with a lust for poker, I know how he won. By instinct. He didn't play poker thinking; he played by heart—the same way he grew his corn. To win. By feeling the power of the cards speak to him. I know because I could do this till my father jinxed my game. My father insisted I think when I played poker. Watch which cards have been thrown he insisted.

"That's not how I play," I tell my father.

"How do you play poker?" he demands to know.

"I feel the cards."

"What do you mean 'you feel the cards'?" he is puzzled.

"I sense what is in my hand and what everyone else has in their hands. I play for aces. I play for face cards. I feel the power of the cards. I know who has what and I play my cards by what they say to me."

My father makes a face at me, disregards what I just told him, and directs me to play by thinking.

50

"I can't play poker that way," I tell dad.

"How else can you play, then?" he is skeptical.

"I know what I know and I know what the next card played will be and I feel my way through the game," I tell him. I feel my confidence slipping. I feel my magic way of playing cards seep out of me. I am ten years old trying to explain to my father that I play poker the way I bet his *papa* played poker. By instinct. By feel of the cards. I can almost hear the deck vibrate on the table. I am not clairvoyant, but I know where the Ace of Spades is and who has the king of spades to beat my queen by the shape of the fan of cards in their hands. I win. My husband plays his hand—straight flush. I lay mine down—royal straight flush. This time we are playing poker in the kitchen in my *pépère*'s house. I smell his spirit as he walks away from me—compost, sandy loam, sulfur from the mill, a fresh pack of cards, old money rubbed by many, and choke cherry wine. My legacy is to play poker. I inherited it from my *pépère* who died with enough money accumulated from playing poker to support his family two years on steak every day for lunch after he died. That was his claim to fame. Corn on the cob for sale by the 4th of July and poker playing to win.

"A very good and enjoyable (we know) public temperance meeting was held in the Universalist Chapel at West Waterville, on Thursday evening. It closed a session of the Templars. Half a dozen fluent and pungent speeches, aimed at different points, kept the audience well entertained up to the time of an early adjournment. By call from the chair, Joshua Nye, Esq., always a favorite speaker in an earnest temperance audience, led in a varied talk, in which the progress of the cause, with its present political bearings and suggestions, was presented in his usual frankness."

—*The Waterville Mail, Vol. XXIV, No. 10, September 2, 1870*

Fluent and Pungent

Last night I went to hear that famous woman writer from Northern Maine with the French last name who claims she's Scotch/Irish. She takes after her *maman*. Like we all do. *Maman*s are important people. Especially to middle-aged orphans such as myself.

I try to think what about me is French. I am confused and I try to pinpoint it. It must be the way I cook. *Maman* always starts her spaghetti by frying salt pork which she leaves to cool and I eat as an after school snack. Fried salt pork rinds. They are my favorite. Deeply browned and crisped. Very salty. I drink tons of water after I eat the fried salt pork. I consider this a delicacy and a very special treat.

My husband and I are in *Québec*—we go to *l'Ile d'Orleans* to search out the ancestors. *Jean Côte*, the one who came across from *Mortagne-au-Perche* in the 1600s is buried there. Along with others. We stop at a restaurant to eat. I see that fried salt pork is on the menu as an appetizer. I go wild. I order some. The waitress is skeptical about my authenticity—like I am not a real princess and I won't feel the pea—or eat the salt pork fried up that's served in a bowl. I lick the platter clean. She has to go back to the kitchen to save face. I take two pieces of the fried salt port with us back to the hotel room to share with my son. He won't even look at the stuff. Another day, I fry some up at home and he eats it like the good, little French boy he is. Getting right in line for a heart attack, too. But for a taste—fried salt pork can be a real treat. *Lard salle* I call it. In Canada, they are called *Oreilles de crisse*. Sounds like Christ's ears to me. Eating fried salt pork in memory of the temple guard who got his ear sliced off by one of Christ's men. It's like the living Bible.

Salt pork is everywhere. Fresh string beans in the pressure cooker with salt pork thrown in *pour donner d'bon goût*. Salt pork

53

in the beans. In the soup. *Soupe aux pois.* Salt pork as a staple. No French-Canadian, later called Franco-American, cook would be caught without the salt pork in her kitchen.

Dad told me how he made his salt pork when he kept pigs. In the cellar, crocks, full of brine and pork sides. Weighted down with a wooden cover to keep the fat from floating to the top. "Why?" I wonder out loud. Sometimes I was an embarrassment to my father by how much of his knowledge I was ignorant of and had no idea I was supposed to have ingested what he knew through the process of being an offshoot of his sperm and my *maman*'s egg.

Growl.

He would growl at me when I didn't know what I was supposed to know. Growl.

I stand there, guilty.

"Because, *bebite*, fat floats," he said.

"Oh."

"Why wouldn't the pork go bad?" I ask.

"Because of the brine," he said "and the root cellar was always cool."

I am a skeptic. "Root cellar?" "Cool."

"*T'sais comment ça faisait tout le temps frais dans l'cave?*" *i'me d'mande.*

"Yes," *je lui réponds.*

"*Bin, c'etait comme ça.* The root cellar was always cool."

"You mean you kept food from spoiling down cellar at *mémère*'s house?"

"*Bin, oui!*" he said emphatically.

"Cool." I'm impressed. I think about the root cellar.

I remember the sandy loam in the floor when I used to go down the narrow steps as a child. The light switch at the top of the stairs was an old-fashioned ceramic-twist-of-the-switch. It was very dark and dank. There were two parts to the basement. One where the furnace was, where the wood was stored and another behind the wide planked wall with a door which led to where the earthen floor kept things cool. The root cellar. To go along with *mémère*'s summer kitchen.

Dad gives me the recipe for the brine. Like I was going to need it soon.

I make a note of the ingredients and method in a general way, but I forget the quantities. Salt, sugar, saltpeter. Water. Glass crocks. And cool storage. O.K. The meat and the salt are layered and then brined.

I cook with salt pork.

I am freshly married. I buy some pork ribs at the grocery store. The meat when cooked gives off some kind of smell which I have never smelt. Surrounded by food all my life and I never took an interest in its properties. Except that it be set before me on the table and I ate it. Now that I'm in charge of the oven's hell gate, I'm a good gatekeeper. What was that smell?

I complained to *maman* and dad about this smell coming off the ribs. It was so strong we threw the meat away and boiled some hot dogs. We ate out on the porch. I almost got sick.

Dad said: "They waited too long to castrate the pig before they slaughtered it."

"No..." said the skeptic. I think: boy he's really lost it this time. Castration and cooking?

"Yes," he is insistent and sure of what he is saying.

"*Maman*, dad says the pork tasted funny because of the pig's balls. Is that true?"

"Oh, yes," she emphasizes the yes to make it sound like "Yeeees." "He ought to know," she says "he slaughtered pigs with his father all the time. And when we were first married. Your father used to keep pigs right where we built the house."

"Pigs are buried all around here," he says.

"*Écoute moé*, if they don't castrate the pig at just the right time, the juice goes all through the meat and makes the meat taste bitter. It would not of hurt you to eat that meat. It tasted funny, that's all."

"It stank!" I protested loudly. "I gagged on the smell."

Then he tells me the proper way to slaughter a pig.

"I had a special mallet," he said, "and I would hit that pig right between the eyes to knock the sonofabitch over." He points to the middle of his own forehead with the middle finger of his left hand. He sits in his chair, leaning back, handling the armrests nervously. His hands never stop.

"Keel right over. With one good blow to the head." He says this and I know it is true. My father was a small man, but he had the strength of a man twice his size. Maybe three men.

"We would string that pig up by his feet with a block and tackle after we had fattened him up nice on corn and slit the troat. I would cut the troat right in the big vein in the neck and drain the blood into a big *chardron* to make some nice blood sausage. *Mon Djieu! c'est assez bon, ça.*" He is not even talking to me anymore, he is in waking REM.

"I had cut the balls off the boy pig and so my pork meat never had that bitter taste you tasted," he is proud. A good farmer. I sit and wrinkle my nose at the sight pig killing must of made. He wants me to know my way around the farm yard. Just in case. Or to give me what he knows. You never know when there will be another Depression.

"Then we would butcher the pig," he explains. "Some nice hams, chops, bacon, and all kinds of good stuff. Out of the head we would make *creton* and then pickled pig's feet."

"Everything but the squeal," he laughs.

"Boy, oh, boy, those pigs knew when it was time to die. They would be so noisy, running around!"

I'm not sure what to think. I can't forget how to make salt pork or how to slaughter a pig. I have all this information and no place to put it. I am *Canuck*, I live in Maine and I cook with salt pork. Dad used to make the salt pork and hams and chops and bacon. I am a cultural dead-end. What am I supposed to do with the lessons he gave me? Who am I supposed to tell the ways of his people? How do his lessons fit in with the way I live?

After *maman* died I took him to the grocery store—this former pig farmer in his spare time when he wasn't working his doubles and triples at the pulp mill—and I was going to show him my fool-proof method of choosing a good cut of meat, always tender in the meat case. I showed him the way that the grain of the meat ran and then how some were so tough you couldn't sink your finger into the muscle. Dad does not get the trick. He slams his thumb down into the meat, instantly breaking through the plastic.

"Boy, you can really tell which piece is tender doing it that way," I say dryly.

"What did I do wrong?" he asks.

"Do it like this," I say, demonstrating restraint.

"Push very softly down on the meat and don't slam your thumb down so hard."

His next try is much better.

"Now," I tell him, "you will never bring home a tough piece of meat again!"

It is his turn to be skeptical.

"First, you choose your price and how much you want to pay."

He was headed toward the 'best cuts' because they were more expensive.

"Money does not mean a more tender piece of meat," I state.

He looks at me with his New York Sirloin in hand.

"Put it back," I tell him, "and come here."

"This one, dad, feels just like butter. See? You can sink your finger into it and it doesn't feel like a tough piece of shoe leather at all. This is the one you want."

"Ça coûte pas cher," i'me dit.

"Price is not how you tell a good piece of meat." I will not be moved from my superior place of knowing.

I tell him how I discovered this method of choosing tender meat. When I was seven or eight years old grocery shopping with *maman*, she would take forever to choose her meat. I would lay my arm on the glass case and then lay my head on my arm and slide along testing all the meats for softness. The redness of the meat looks beautiful and luscious to me. I cannot stop looking at the beauty of the red cow meat. I am enthralled by how good the meat looks. Raw. I could eat it on the spot. I stare and I sense a blood lust in me. I am mesmerized by the look of all the rawness. I lay my head on the case and I stare at the meat. The meat in the butcher's case at Ted's corner market is even better looking. I see *Armand*'s blood-stained apron and his hands which he wipes on it. I take my time walking by the meat case. I walk slow. I stare and I lean. *Maman* goes on to do her shopping, but I stay with the meat and I touch its softness. Rejecting the toughness. She tells me, "Don't touch the meat." or "Don't break the plastic." I touch the meat. I break the plastic. All along the meat case are finger prints and holes in the plastic where I have gone along and touched and touched and touched.

"Sojourner Truth, the famous old colored woman, gave her testimony in Providence against the women she saw on the stage at the Women's Suffrage Convention the other day, I thought what kind of reformers be you, with goose wings on your head as if you were going to fly, and dressed in such ridiculous fashion, talking about reform and women's rights? 'Pears to me you had better reform yourselves first."
—*The Waterville Mail, Vol. XXIV, No. 20, November 11, 1870*

'Pears To Me

Where I come from is where I want to be. I used to want to come from somewhere else. I pretend myself in some other context. More white. I am a Franco-American girl growing up in a French-Canadian neighborhood. *Un p'tit Canada*. Rumor has it that we give out sex for free. Like candy. We have a reputation of being uninhibited. We have body language, but what we Franco-American girls are saying isn't what the Colby boys and *"les anglais"* are hearing. Things get confused. The Colby guys take a ride down our street to pick up some women. Not so they can fall in love and marry them and things like that. We side-step them on the sidewalk. Things are less formal in the sixties, but the scent of superiority coming off Mayflower, ha!, Hill is still the same. All things flow toward the river in those days before waste treatment plants— so down on Water Street we had twice the amount to deal with— our own and the stuff flowing down in attitudes from up on the Hill.

Body language is an art. Body language is a code. Body language is a secret. Take leaning for example. French women lean. They lean on lamp posts when they talk to the guys. Leaning is sex standing up, but leaning is a casualness of posture, too. I lean because I am tired. Women who lean are inviting with their bodies to do some other kinds of leaning. We French girls can lean and not mean what the leaning says. Dad or *maman* would kill them. Repression goes a long way in a strict, Catholic neighborhood. There is leaning because you are tired and there's leaning-with-intent toward someone else. I was leaned toward by a priest once. A priest leaning against a post at a dance despite his tight, white collar stuck in his breast pocket, looking like a toughie dressed in black. The collar resembles a tongue depressor sticking out of his pocket. Something suggestive or subliminal. "Poor devils," *maman* says about the priests. She knows they lack leaning in their lives. She understood their loneliness. Despite her unhappiness in her marriage, she felt their sacrifice was much more sorrowful. "That's no kind of life," she says. "Always alone." Same thing for the nuns. Whenever I come home and tell her I think I want to be a nun, *maman* would say: "Oh, my God. Have they been brainwashing you again? Do you want to be lonely all your life? That's no way to live." "Get outa here...you don't want to be a nun." I go back to parochial school and be silent whenever the nuns start to tell us about their lives of wonderful sacrifice. Don't we hear the Call? The Call? Don't we know in our hearts Jesus wants us to be just like them? Holy and good. I sit there silent and feeling like a traitor, but I know what *maman* will say if I tell her I want to be a nun.

"You don't know what you want," she said. "Those people never had a life. They go into the convent when they are very young, never went out on a date, never kissed a man, never can leave the convent. Their mother's funeral passes right in front of the convent and they cannot even go to the church. Get outa here. Don't tell me you want to be a nun."

So I sit when they talk about being a nun. I put on a very-interested-in-what-you-are-saying face and pray that they shut up pretty soon. I nod appropriately, like the fake I am. The other girls, the teacher's pets, the first, second and third chair girls, sometimes the fourth chair girl, too, all say they will be nuns. I sit in the back and say nothing. I am asked. "Are you thinking of being a nun?" they ask, diplomats for chairs-in-the-front and teacher's pets anonymous. "I'm thinking," I tell them.

Maman, at least, has someone to fight with and then, there were the times when things were O.K. between her and dad. Like when they work on their flowers together. Or their lawns. The place where I come from, *chez-nous*, looks like a park. People would walk down the street from their hot, third floor apartments with their babies to let them run around on our lawn and around the pond dad had dug and piped water to from the stream in the woods running off the cemetery. It was their place of calm. And beauty. How ironic. All I want to do is run away from there and get myself another identity. I want to be a white girl. A girl from Mayflower Hill. A girl with an English name. An English identity. An English sexuality. An English sensibility. An English everything. Instead, I have French as French could be. I want straight legs and not the bulgy kind I was born with. I hate my legs. They embarrass me. Curvy. Big calves. Like baby cows on a girl. Everyone laughs at me when I tell them. *Maman*, too. They hoot. "You'll find out..." they sing-song. "What!" I wonder, mourning my funny looking legs.

And the feet, the feet have got to go. Peasant feet, that's what these things are. Feet that have walked barefoot in the garden for centuries. Bunions from ages past. A whole history of a people written on these ugly, ugly feet. I look at *maman* and dad's feet and I see that my chances for pretty feet are not so good. Hers are just as ugly as his, but for some reason I blame him for my feet.

"Gee, thanks, dad, for the ugliest feet in the world," I say to him. "Look at your ugly feet!" I exclaim, wailing. "How did they get so bad?" I want to know the whole story of his mutilation and in it may be a clue as to why my feet are so bad looking as well. Some kind of foot binding torture on our side of the world?

"I wore bad shoes," he says. "Inexpensive shoes."

What kind of shoes would deform feet to that extent? Consequently, I have good shoes bought for me at the most expensive store in town. I can only wear sneakers in the summer. No support. Ruin your feet. How can you ruin already ruined feet? In gym, or Girl Scout Camp I see English-speaking girls with pretty feet. Straight toes. No bunions. I am on a campaign to straighten out my feet. I walk barefoot all summer to straighten out my toes. I concentrate on one foot. I am only fifteen. My bones are still soft from my baby life which is not too, too far away because I have fresh memory of being two still, so I can straighten out my toes.

The pointed shoe era is still here. It's the sixties. Woodstock is next summer. I will hear about it on the radio and wonder how can so many people hear about a concert and show up. I am barely aware of it while it is happening. My feet take up all my attention. I want pretty, English-speaking-girl feet. Not French-speaking-girl peasant feet.

"Julia *Paradis*, a French woman, wife of Frederick *Paradis*, was found dead on the road between Bangor and Oldtown on Tuesday. She was a woman somewhat addicted to the use of strong drink, and though the affair seemed enveloped in mystery, the verdict of the jury, after hearing evidence, was, that she came to her death from exposure to the storm or from cause unknown."
—*The Waterville Mail, Vol. XXV, No. 20, March 24, 1871.*

On The Road Between

I get the idea of going away from my French beginnings when
I do go away from them. I move to a farm in Detroit, Maine. I go to
the four-room schoolhouse and there are boys in the classroom all
the way to the eighth grade. Cute boys. English speaking boys. Some
with French last names and some with German last names, but
they are all farm boys here. Or live next to farms.

Dad wants a farm. He is trying to get better. Dealing with his
depression. His *maman* dying the year before adds to his confu-
sion. This is the time just before the shock treatments. For years,
every Sunday, on *prenait une ride sur les terres*. We go for rides
on the farm. We are looking to buy a farm. Dad is a farmer by heart.
Or by memory. French people eat dirt. He can tell what a soil needs
by touch. A little lime. A little potash. A little more fertilizer. *Un
p'tit peu d'ça.* We all pile into the car and go for rides on the farm.
Sydney. Oakland. Winslow. Albion. The Forks. Benton. Clinton.
Burnham. Vassalboro. Augusta. Finally, Detroit.

Whoever left France in our ancestry in the 1600s, left with the
idea that they were going to get themselves a farm. A collective
memory. On to *Québec* and its stubborn, rock-ridden earthen crust.
Still moving, coming south to New England. French-speakers loose
in a place of discontent. To work in the mills. To keep from starv-
ing. To earn a living and then to go back to the farms in *Québec*
and a way of being which is French. Sort of. Someone lost the map
of France. In my family. *Memère, maman's maman,* used to say
she thought some of our people came from France. We all spoke
French. Someone lost the history book or never wrote one either.
Me, I was just plain leaving the whole thing behind me and I was
going to be an *Améritchaine* girl. Marry me some *améritchain.*
Live in a big white house. Be perfect. No curls in my hair. No leaning allowed. Except I do lean, because I forget. My butt sticks out

when I lean. I am vaguely aware of my posture and what it says. Sometime I want my body saying what I cannot say with my mouth. One boy gets what I say.

I want body language gone, kaput. Get rid of all that junk. My French accent is the first to go. The kids in Detroit, some strawberry blond, pink-faced, freckled girl made fun of my "mudder," "faddur," "choo cherity tree Water Street," so I pretend I am from Boston. My brother is gone to college there. I practice when we bring him. Crash course in accents. I listen to Bostonians and I imitate. Kid power. I learn overnight. I make it up. Shut-up, yer egnoraaant. I drink tonic instead of sodee.

Losing oneself is hard to do. Hard work. Remaking a girl into another girl is tough work. Being white, and *Améritchaine*, not French, Franco-American, is snob work. I become a snob. I ditched my father because his threes will always be trees. *Maman* is not so low class. Her threes are threes. She dresses nice when she goes uptown. *On monte au fort,* we always say. Going up to the fort for supplies. Like I'd been doing it for centuries. Except this is the 1950s and 60s. I walk away from myself. I'm on a road not to self-discovery, but to forgetfulness. Drop all that French stuff and pick up a squeaky clean, fake front of English tea cup society on the highway to hell bound for nowhere. My neighborhood gives me away. To some, I am cheap trash no matter what I do. I am a "Water Street Girl and you know what they are like..." Even the Summer Street French boys say that. They live one tier up from the river, no actually two. The first tier is no longer inhabited. The second tier on this small town five layer cake is Water Street, the next ridge of the ancient riverbed is Summer Street, on par with the same ridge that the cemetery sits on and then you have Silver St. and Main St. level where you continue to climb onto where the air is thin and rare until you hit the Cool St. ridge before you reach Mayflower and Colby Hill. Mount Merici and Cherry Hill Drive are up there too. The French have infiltrated all the levels in this town.

Depending on how much upward mobility your family was into.

Nobody fucks on Mayflower Hill. Not their daughters, anyway. Or so the legend goes. Only Water Street girls fuck. And give crabs. That's what Water Street girls are like. The Chez Paris. Local bar, sometimes a grill and a strip joint. Therefore, we all bump and grind. Ethnic women, debased by sight.

The men who go to Colby are warned to bring condoms when they visit our neighborhood. To visit the nurse's office if anything funny shows up on their skin. Pricks. Some Lolitas, looking for love, give in or out depending on your beliefs, do get recycled. My brothers have this thing about French Virgins. They need a personal sacrifice for the sin of our being French. So I am not approached. Not by Colby guys, anyway. It is their illusion of sanctification. My sexuality is a discussed topic. "Côté! Go get your sister!" "You go near my sister, you baaastard, and I'll kill you," my brother tells him calmly. They know how he feels. So I am unapproached by the neighborhood guys, too. I feel as if someone sprayed an extra can of Raid when I walk on the sidewalk. The guys clear a path. I am high on my power until I find out why they let me pass.

Although I am approached by your garden variety of sex offender on any given day. There is some kind of other way of being in operation here. I am warned about the strange men. Depending which season it is, I have my pick to fend off. Something about expressing sexuality is very different in this neighborhood. Some old men leech. Other old men in the neighborhood don't leech and are fixtures, characters of a time long-spent in these parts. *Souris*. The Candy Man. *Danse-pour-moé*. It is the only name we know him by and what he does. It is a request. As children we play with him. He loves to dance. We know this. We appreciate his pleasure. We hide in the bushes and yell out our request, *"Danse pour moé!"* He stops on the sidewalk, dead drunk, with music playing in his head and dances a dance of light-footed joy. Like a bar of music measures out a routine. He stops and walks a few feet until we call out again. "*Danse pour moé*!" He dances and dances moving sporadically up the street. We play with him. We watch his dance in fascination. I wish I could move like that. So some men wouldn't harm us at all. Those we know.

We know the others, too. The ones who do more than just lean. They do fuck. Or, aspire to fucking. Leer. This is urban—small time stuff, but the men lurk just the same. A beat up, always down on their luck kind of man. Operating on their own rules. Not allowed to play in the Mayflower game. Not even worthy of scrubbing the toilets on Colby Hill. Or, like *m'tante* Annie, amused by the sexual antics of "those college kids." Disgusted by *les moudgits tchuls, m'tante* Annie, hot after a day's work, says, "oh some of those girls are sweethearts, call me *maman* and treat me nice, but some of those rigs, well, I wouldn't want my girl up there with some of those boys. *Les moudgits faces.*" Married by age sixteen, one of the oldest of *mémère*'s seventeen, *m'tante* Annie has very little patience with those spoiled brats—except she understands their youthfulness, the one she never had. "You are married a long time," she always forewarned. Keep away she meant. Take your time to get married. I didn't. I married soon after my eighteenth birthday to another eighteen year old whose mother had to sign for him. "Take your time. You are married for life."

I sit in the classroom with the nuns. They talk Jesus. Joseph. Mary. Heaven. Hell. Holy Communion. The Baltimore Catechism. They talk sacrifice as a way of life where your reward will be great in heaven. Snort. *Maman* always insulted God when she was mad at him about her life's situation. She sing-songed, sarcastic, whining: "Your reward will be great in heaven...how about a little reward down here, Jesus! Jesus. Jesus. Jesus. *La moudgits vie.*" From the convent, I walk home. Depending on what the season is, I am side-swiped sexually. Visual confrontations. If I knew then what I know now, I could have told the men, containing myself: "Your gaze is hitting the side of my face." Then, well, then all I said were

68

very highly crafted insults and looks that could kill. I practice before the mirror. Snort. Sneer, snarl. Sniff. Slowly look sideways at the crawling vermin and say with some effort at stooping to their level, drawling under my breath some remark of supreme disgust. One of my personal favorites is: "Drop dead." Long on the "o" sound for effect. Curt, too. Certainly, disrespectful of the old men. The really old men. Like the thirty or forty year olds. There was no one around to protect me so I taught myself a way of killing without touching. They would crawl back into the holes from which they had come. We had our daily routines. They stole from me visually, at age twelve or thirteen, and I sharpened my verbal claws on their hides. I was quite ignorant of the sex act in reality, I could only sense their hands on me in places I would not take kindly to being touched. It would call for a swift kick to you-know-where or a bite, sink my teeth in, dirty fighting my brother would chide, any place I could get a hold onto and spit in the face, a real clammer in the eye. Two spits maybe. I go through this tunnel of leering doms, dirty old men, every day at 3:00 o'clock. It would happen in the Spring, two brothers, woods cutters who came down from *Québec* and who would stop watching TV long enough to come up onto the street to watch me walk by. My eyes narrow to a slit and I literally spit at them. They laugh and go back downstairs to their basement apartment. I am so good at what I do that after one season of my dirty looks in return, only one brother persists in coming to the street level to view me. The other is shamed into reality. *"T'as pas honte, toé?"* He has no shame. I would swear, too. Under my breath. *"Moudgits, Crisse de Tabadnac."* Goddamned, christly tabernacle. Guess I told him. Tomorrow the nuns will tell me how I am a temple of God and I should keep myself pure. Maybe the nuns haven't been to the temple lately. Have they seen how many people go to the temple? Can I borrow your habit so I can walk home, *chère*? Here, let me pinch your cheek till the skin comes off in my hand like you always do, too, *Mere de Bonne Conscience*.

"Management of Brooms—If brooms are wet in boiling suds once a week they will become very tough, will not cut the carpet, last much longer, and always sweep like a new broom. A very dusty carpet maybe cleansed by setting a pail of cold water out by the door, wet the broom in it, knock it to get off all the drops, sweep a yard or so, then wash the broom as before and sweep again, being careful to shake all the drops off the broom and not sweep far at a time."

—*The Waterville Mail, Vol. XXV, No. 19, November 4, 1870*

Far At A Time

There are some thoughts you can entertain for days because they are like candy to the brain. Sweet, sweet thoughts. Resting easy on your mind, you lie in them for the sheer pleasure of their silkiness. Soft and flowing thought patterns; brain waves in undulation across the sea of synapse. And then someone slams a door or comes into the room asking where the cat's flea powder is or can you help me find the can opener (it's hanging under the cupboard) because I want to cook. Cook is opening a can of ravioli. I'm impressed. Gourmet cooking is macaroni and cheese that comes in a box. *Maman* is rolling over several times in her grave. I sit and stitch the quilted coats in echo of the land. I think of all the quilts I've seen and I recognize these quilts in the earth's patterns while in flight from Bangor, Maine to Lafayette, Louisiana. I'm going to see a friend and look at some roots or something like roots in Louisiana. I've been to Canada and France, now I'm going to see the Diaspora in Louisiana. There are *Côtes* everywhere.

"It's like a treasure hunt for you?" my airline seatmate inquires. Earlier he looked at me and remarked: "You don't look like no coonass." I'm looking at him, "What's a coonass?" His treasure hunt remark was a way of saving face.

"Coonass?" I am puzzled. I can just about guess what he is saying although.

"You know," he says.

I shake my head no.

"That's what they call the Frenchies down in Louisiana. Coonasses." he informs me. I am not amused. He can tell. So he switches to the buried treasure routine.

"Yes," I smile to myself. A treasure hunt. How can I miss when looking for buried culture? I can't. How does he, as a perfect stranger, as only strangers can be perfect, know or feel the need and the joy of exploring deeper depths of the self. A few questions from him; statements, explanations from me and he instinctually knows the importance of my sojourn to Louisiana.

In Memphis, four small children run to meet their mother—screaming, happy, one yells, "new shoes!" They are all over her. "Bright, shiny, new shoes," he yells. Kids know their mother's lives like a well-traveled land of their own. I am thinking of my own children, who used to be small, and when I was their port of call. It is one of the silky thoughts I keep with me, even though some days I felt like a stevedore.

I forgot that we crossed another time zone. I thought I was going to miss my connecting flight. I had a chance to live 2:30 all over again. We flew south and now we are turning right. *Mon Djieu!* The land below is exquisite! I wish I were a quilt artist. The land is so beautiful I would copy its patterns in quilt. And then I think, I have already. Unknowingly. It is from 10,000 feet in the air and the vantage point of flight that I recognize that I have echoed the patterns of the earth in cloth and quilt. And so haven't all the other quilters—all the other women who piece cloth in response to the land on which they live. How can we have come to the conclusion of cloth repeating the patterns of the earth? How can the women of bygone eras, without the aid of flight know how far-reaching their quilt patterns vibrated in tune to the patchwork of the earth? Or is this one of those times when everybody knew but me?

"There's power in those quilts," a friend once said to me. "Why do you suppose everyone wants to have one or to get their hands on the family quilts?" I stand there wide-eyed, rooted, remembering. Caskets and quilts.

In flight, I write a poem in honor of the quilt:

The View From Flight 5410—Northwest—Memphis-to-Lafayette

What is a quilt?
A quilt is a woman's garden
fields of cloth
echoing the earth
harrowing—plowing
seeding
weeding
reaping
repeating
the gifts
first fruits
forests
groves
crazy quilt fluvial plains
snaking rivers.
geological fossils
road bed
farm labor
cain raising cain
swirling sweeping
river bed
bound to the river
to the oceans
to the sea.
raised threads
borders between
field & forests
crazy quilt
ordered pattern
a cloud's shadow
belongs.

shadings
gradations
"in search of our
mother's gardens"
grown
in cloth
quilting
earth-bound
echoing
repeating
the meter, measure
of the land—
pull the clouds
from the sky
cotton batting
fluff
  stuffed

_____

Quilt
earth &
  sky
unite.

_____

"There's power in those quilts," she warned me. I simply nodded
yes.

"Excursions.—...The Lightfoot Base Ball Club, of West Waterville accompanied the first excursion and played a friendly game with the Katahdins of Dexter, beating them in a score of 33 to 30."
—*The Waterville Mail, Vol. XXV, No. 8, August 19, 1870*

Excursions

I lost the threads of the dream. I dropped the stitches of a whole evening's work. In my lap. Like I was only fooling around and dreaming all night long without meaning a single thing that went on in my mind. The world of the upside down, the prides of clouds casting their shadows onto us creating shade. Dreams cast similar shadows as clouds creating shade. Like memory which is really manifestation of who we are today. The accumulation of lived lives playing itself out daily in gesture, remark and habit. The original blueprint or intent lost through the years. How old is that habit of mine when I stand there in a stance which screams out my *maman* and her habits. Familial postures. Expressions of origins like a map telling us where we came from and where we are going. Each one an accomplice of our fingerprints.

We inhale our dead. Or we ingest their manners. I am sitting eating my supper with one elbow on the table. "You sit at the table just like your father did," my husband calmly remarks. "Why do you do that?" he asks, curious. I've had a highball. I sneeze every time I drink just like dad did.

"I know I am doing that," I reply, "I'm not sure why I do it." It is a habit I acquired after he died. Is this my way of being with my father? To become him in posture. I am acting out an obligation or a privilege. It feels like both. I study my aunt's hands waving or coming to rest as a bird in flight while she talks or sits there. I am doing research on body language of the family women. Who am I when my body speaks? With certain aspects of the body language lost in me I feel like a modern fraud. Like there is a fashion in body motions such as there is in popular dance. Franco-American women in their families and communities have signature gestures that signal silent speech. Certain things mean certain things. I understand the language well, but I don't always speak it. Movable body parts

76

speech coming off ethnics scares the pants off the non-participating other ethnics—in Maine, the body speakers would be the Franco-Americans, French-Canadians, or French heritage types and the non-body speakers would be the non-French heritage types. "Me," I say tapping my own chest with the right hand's middle finger, "me," repeating for emphasis both the word and the motion, "I am a French heritage type." *Canuck.* I sometimes get my signals confused.

In a Laundromat in France I watched with grave interest three people, a man and two women, talk about some renovations they were planning together about the Laundromat. Three large people stood in a three-foot square floor space, faces pressed close, yelling, gesticulating, arms flailing, hands waving, pointing, tapping chest, palm splaying and retreating, only to begin this commonplace-in-France drama of intense conversational exchanges all over again. No one was angry. Just passionate. Intense. Body languaging. Telling story their way. I am no stranger to this kind of conversation and I am looking for Mr./Mrs./Ms. Good Body Language everywhere. After a century or two of being suppressed, whenever I hear someone speaking with an original body accent, I want to pin a medal of bravery on their chest. Prejudice is a good teacher of conformity. If that is your goal in life.

We had moved to Detroit, Maine, in search of my father's collective memory of "*sur les terres.*" He was looking for the "Good Farm." I attended the four-room village school. My brother told me, "you are going to *Die* in *Die*troit." The locals pronounced the place: DEEtroit. While making fun of their pronunciation, he meant the place was boring; what really happened was worse than being bored.

"You talk with your hands," Sue in the pink-checkered dress, strawberry-blond tells me at age eleven.

"Oh, yeah? What did I just say?" I quip.

77

"You must be French," she accuses.

"You must be a genius," I sneer. I had told them all at this school I was French. Maybe this wasn't such a good idea I am finding out. Considering her loose reputation she has gathered for herself by age eleven, if we put child prostitution and being French on the same level of social outcasts, and often that is the case, I didn't think she, the slut, not being French herself, but free with her new tits with the farm boys, had much to crow about. I was going to tell her how cheap she was giving away her breasts for free, but I thought of how deep this would hit and hurt so I swallow my words and glare out the window. I am hurt by her remarks about my being French. She doesn't stop there, miss-can-I-sit-on-your-lap-so-you-can-feel-me-up. She laughs at how I pronounce my words. How I speak. She repeats the sounds I make. Sing-song. Counter-sneering. Screwing up her face.

"You don't want to keep your face looking like that too long," I tell her, "it may be permanent."
My next insult has to do with body odor. I got this one from my big brother. I'm not quite sure I know its exact meaning, but I say it anyway.

"Do you always smell that way?" I remark, "Or don't you ever wash?"

"Thoo-turty-tree Water Street," she replies. "Turdy, turdy, turdy, turd." In other words, I'm shit.

"Your mudder and your fadder," she crows. I stand there muted. For the first time in my life, I hear how I sound to other people because my first language was French. I am eleven years old.

"You're just jealous because I can speak French and you can't." This was my last attempt. This insult comes from my *maman* telling me how the other boys would laugh at my brothers pushing me around the neighborhood in Waterville in the baby carriage. They would just laugh back and say to the boys, "You're just jealous because you don't have a baby sister to push around in the baby carriage." So I was a Madame Queen in a Carriage viewing my kingdom just as my daughter was a generation later in Deering Oaks Park . Sue was just jealous. That's it. She was jealous, but it wasn't because of my accent. I figured it out why she was jealous later on. Some boy liked me and not her. The most popular boy. The cutest boy. The sexiest boy. The most daring boy. The most blue-eyed, crow-black haired boy.

Sue hooted. "Of being a dumb Frenchman? HA!" She walks away in her pink gingham checkered dress which was too tight with her so-called famous breast the size of walnuts. Her too-tight perm, cut too short flying on her head. After that, I stayed in the classroom all winter during all recesses to read. I read sixty books that winter which I bought with my allowance I earned working in the chicken barn. Almost the complete set of *Nancy Drew* mysteries. *Trixie Belden. Donna Parker.* Mysteries are my favorites. And I read all the bookmobile books I could lay my hands on. I hardly open my mouth to speak. I'm working on a new accent in secret. A Boston accent. I'm practicing Bostonian speech patterns in my girl brain and come spring I no longer say "thoo-turty-tree" or "mudder and fadder." I enunciate and pronounce my words as if I had chewed them forty times each. I lived at Two-Thirty-Three Water Street with my Mother and Father. Very tea cup. Except we never use saucers when we drink coffee or tea *chez-nous.* And, cool. I have new insults which I picked up while in Boston. "Shut up, yer ignorant," or "Hey! Hey! Not interested," or when someone was being a pest— "You want to call off your dogs?" I used these special insults for years. Even today. Sometimes someone will ask me: "Do you come from Boston?" I just shudder and laugh to myself. Should I send myself a sympathy card for dying in Dietroit or what?

"BUANDERIE DE FALL RIVER! FALL RIVER LAUNDRY, No. 24, rue Hartwell, Collette et manchettes, 2 cents, pièce tapis battus et nettoyés à la vapeur, 4 cents la verge. Linge lavé, empesé, repassé ou non, au grès des clients. On va chercher sans frais tous les paquets à domicile..."

—*L'Indépendant,* 4ième année, No. 3 Foi, loyauté, progrès, Fall River, Mass, 20 janvier, 1888

Collette et manchettes, 2 cents

Perfect, present, future tense. In French. Everything in French. Even if it is in English, it is still in French. A layer of French living laid over by layers of popular culture or popular culture covered by living done in French. Intertwined. I wish I had a happier story to tell, but I've made my peace with its ugliness. It is a truthful, unpretty face. I have learned to love the story I hated. One of the deep reverberations that I must reacquaint myself with. Legends. Customs. Recipes. Folktales. Stories. Songs. Futuristic visions. I have visions of perfect, present, future tense. What am I in the future of my Franco-American womaning? Do I learn the language? Do I write my way to freedom? Will I be understood by even myself, I wonder, let alone someone without a cultural blueprint. I am scared. Afraid of the outcome. The judgments. The pronouncements. Some have more of the inner sanctum secret passwords than others. Some have the original recipes. Some can sing. Some know the essence of the moment told in French words. I can hear the heartbeat of *Québec*. I can hear the St. Lawrence River, *le fleuve St. Laurent* running in my bloodstream. I am giant and I have out of the body experiences picking up tankers on the St. Lawrence looking down from the 13th floor of *Le Concorde*. I eat the soup, bread, *plat principal*, and desert without a bit of explanation necessary. I climb on my knees the prayer stairs at *Ste. Anne de Beaupré*. I am close to *Jean Côte*'s grave on *l'Île d'Orléans*. He arrived just yesterday— 1600 something. I married the very distant cousin. I eat the soup. I bake the bread. I am a *couseuse*. I make bold the colors in my house. I get dizzy admiring the roofs in *Québec*. The colors on the houses leave me breathless. I have been shamed to white, but I vow to return to the palette of true colors. I dream the visions of young women in French. Equanimity in the cultural unearthing of their legacy of the near millennium. Do-it-to-yourself archaeology.

The cookbook of life rendered for what it is. That which sustains the generations to come. Pride, not shame in the female cook pot. Modern day tapestry of living unparalleled in its boasts. *On parle français, ici* the commercial advertisements read. Understood, at last.

I talk about losing a piece of one's body and it is like losing a piece of one's self in their culture. Changed forever, but you continue to live just the same. You take it all in stride. I chose to tattoo pressed flowers over my mastectomy scar. Just like in the poster made famous by the woman depicting the female crucifixion, salvation for all, in the skyline pose. Naked to the waist, outdoors and celebrating single-breastedness. Culture women, Franco-American women, in the folds of nature and the future, celebrating the newly designed and defined selves. That present, future, tense. Maybe, not perfect, but who would want it?

Am I willing to give more weight to the dark side of story rather than the good side of story—although the dark is as necessary as the light. It is my fears which interfere. Because in each story is the light and the dark. The evil and the good.

I want to tell someone something and one day I need to tell it from over here with that day's rations of embellishments, and then the next day I have a different view of what I want to say about the same thing because I've changed and I've become better seasoned in my own passage through the personal truths. I can understand the event in a different light. I am impressed with what I choose to tell and what I choose to not tell and then when I tell the story, how it sometimes doesn't even come close to what it is I experienced or what happened. Words are slippery. Slimy. Gooey. Slick. Silky. A breath of air on the wind. Utterances echoing. I am struck with what a story is about. (The Franco-American and Acadian festivals in the summer whispering our fame.) Usually not what actually took place because people have a way of not corroborating their stories. (Everyone's recipe for *tourtière* is different.) They

need to tell their version to protect their interests. (Stewed tomatoes as signature.) Or, they just cannot tell a good story or put the right words to the experience. (Immigration as person
denied in a land of forget who you were, you're here now story.) Whoever they are writing or telling the story to does not have the time or the patience to listen to them. They tell the long version when a shorter version could be said. (How do you spell your name mill boss says to M. *Poulin*, the non-reader and non-writer. P-O-O-L-E-R, the mill boss tells him.)

When you draw it is a matter of seeing more than a matter of moving the pencil or charcoal to do what you want. Some skill of the hand is needed to record the seeing, but it is in the seeing the thing drawn is recorded. The event of a tree standing there in all its glory of autumn. The river coming into focus for the duration of the winter months as the leaves shed their camouflage and the river's disappearing act in the Spring of the year when the trees regain their composure of leaves once again. (Reclaiming one's right to one's culture and singing one's songs. The forces of tradition blowing against the shores of modernity. What flashes across your mind is the view of dancers dancing the gigues while you shop the aisles in the grocery store. The women all around you speak in French or *Franglais*. They say the French culture is dead. Are these people ghosts?) Regeneration. The sign of nature to us that we too are hopefuls in possibilities of becoming new people.

To write, is to see. To record. To believe in the belonging to the telling. To express. To explain. (Even if only to oneself.) Acquire. Words are paint. Words as picture. Dad always said "one picture is worth a thousand words." It is only one picture and a thousand words are a thousand words with the possibility of multiplication, proliferation, exponential growth because of their suggestive lucidity.

So we tell and re-tell. Telling has nothing to do with competing. Or being beat down because the telling does not match the criteria of some other kind of telling. (*No Adam in Eden* by Grace Metalious or *Canuck* by *Camille Lessard Bissonnette* telling.) Telling is its own story and its own reward. The story has its birth in our way of being and not to doubt our experience just because someone has a formula for themselves and their story. My story is of me as I represent the *grandmères'* bloodline. (Raining down through the centuries like crashing waves of consciousness coming to being. When I walked the streets of Angers, France I did not know that the woman immigrant who began the line of women on my *maman*'s side lived here centuries before.)

Like I can remember the curve in the road which I can see from my windows in my house with all the years I've looked out onto the road with my thoughts. Thinking of my *maman*'s death, my father's death, the years of traffic going by, the seasons changing under my gaze, the steeples visible in the distance, my children, my brothers and their lives. My brother's death. Me, as a young *maman*, as a cancer patient, with my husband coming home on that road. The train tracks which cross the road's path. The yellow lines newly painted, and fading with the passing time and traffic. I stand in the house, and the road has not moved or changed, but yet I see the road very differently now than when I first lived here with my hopes set on high. Sorry, but that is not the way the bend in the road goes. The road is resolute and real. (One million *Québécois* immigrated to the Northeast between the years 1820 and 1920 all with descendants today living in the entire Northeast.) It is me standing at the window looking at its curve imposing my meaning on the view. My thoughts floating heavenward, becoming golden letters in the book of life.

Like the heartbeat, no matter what, passed on from generation to generation. I have the French language and the French way of being in Maine. A historical me. One who was born into a life. Lives. Moving toward the white light that sucks up the soul. We are full of smells in our souls of those things which we live with in our lifetimes. That is why our sense of smell is so acute. Like our eyes which are windows into our soul, our sense of smell is how we find our way home. (The frenzied supper hour. The salt-porked beans.) Our five senses are like the petals of a star in the heavens, or a star fish on the beach, or the inside of an apple cut to reveal its inner heart's core of truth star. Our own five-pointed starness of head and limbs echo the central being of unity to which we all belong in relation to the other five-pointed beings and their placement. Their constancy of change in the sky. Who we are when we move together. The five senses are our points of being inside of the other physically five appendages. We are all stars. All *vedettes*. In our own universes. We are entities and parts of constellations.

Living does a little twisty dance all over expectations and the story changes from the one you have in your head. (I will be French in Maine, Franco-American female, and proud of it.) So it all becomes more story. Or song. Lamentations. War wounds. Epitaph. What we choose to see when we look is what is really there—disappointment and celebration. We can remain aloof, outside, cold, indifferent; or we can belong, praise, recognize, sing alleluias. We can reject. Accept at will. Disagree with. Affirm. We belong to the story plane much like we belong to the picture plane. Depth of field and focus. Good lighting. Bad lighting. Shadow. Sun. Dark. The shifting sands of conversing. Telling. Storying. Each one comes to us and we are filters of the future. We decide what will be seen and heard only so much as we carefully choose the words which do the telling.

For someone to doubt the telling or to devalue the telling of a story makes telling difficult for the one doing story. And also for the one who refuses a story's life. Clear, careful, concise. Clean. With a mind to multiple views of the same view. And the passing years. That is how we tell a story. That is how we become future.

Fin

Epilogue

THE EDUCATION OF WOMEN—H.C. Dane Esq., has been lately contributing to one of our leading journals some thoughtful considerations in reference to this topic...The arguments adduced by the writer alluded to are appalling and the worst thing about it is they are true. Take the matter of dress for example:

Paris gives woman her style of dress. Paris, with its idea of female virtue: Paris, with its female license and abandonment; Paris, with its legalized system of prostitution, gives Christian America its style of female dress, which is studied for one great purpose— to fascinate the eyes and arouse the passions of men...It is plain, then, if we would remove the social evil we must first signalize its causes and remove them, not only by penal enactment but the introduction of a truer and more Christian education of the sex.

—*The Waterville Mail, Vol. XXIV, No. 23 December 2, 1870*

Not Only By Penal Enactment

A parable according to Water Street:

So again, we are arguing with God. Where the hell are you? And what is the point of taking such a long coffee break? Where the hell can we find you? Strap us down with these puny needs or appetites while you go off to be cool and be God. Running the universe, you say? Why can't you do it from here or where we can see you? To keep the lobbyist off your back. So you can think more clearly? Test run for eternity, you say? A little housekeeping detail?

Jesus as Man? If you were a truly brave God, Jesus could have been Josephine. Except the first time she spoke **She** would have been crucified. At once! Pharisees were afraid of Jesus. Afraid he'd make more like him. Sent the temple whore down to check it out. 'Cept she had a foot fetish. Fell in love 'cause Jesus wasn't a bad-looking boy, and he had had experience with an adulteress and sand writing. He knew who that woman had been with. Knew the man's name—was writing it in the sand. Big, local mob boss. Everybody owed him some money or was getting a cut in his deals. No one had the cash ready and they wanted their cash flow to remain lucrative so they decided to let the mob boss' woman live. Just some funky chick up from Jerusalem anyway. She was leaving town next week. No need to upset the mob boss. They began to give their excuses: Gotta go get supper! Horse needs feed. I need new shoes. My mother's calling me. I have to go pee. I've lain with her myself. Maybe Jesus will write my name in the sand next. Let's go, wife. We're wasting our time. Bra strap broke. See ya. No one was left. Jesus wipes out the mob boss's name. Where did they all go? She knew about Jesus from Mary M, so she just smiled. We, adulteresses talk, too, she thinks. Jesus says: Have a nice day. Walks away. Everyone thinks he said, "Go and sin no more." But Jesus was not interested in her sins, but her saving soul. She was worth more alive than dead. Everyone who saw her would remember. Go and sin no more. So her name got to be Godisinnomore. Shortened to Goddess. Sister to Jesus.

About the author

Côté Robbins was brought up bilingually in a Franco-American neighborhood in Waterville, Maine known as 'down the Plains'. Her *maman* came from Wallagrass, a town in the northern part of the state and her father was from Waterville. She has spent many years researching the origins and visiting the hometowns of her ancestors in Canada and France.

Côté Robbins was the winner of the Maine Chapbook Award for her work of creative nonfiction entitled, *Wednesday's Child*. She is a founder and Executive Director of the Franco-American Women's Institute. She has written a sequel titled 'down the Plains.'

She lives in Brewer with her husband, David. They have three grown children.

Other books by Rhea Côté Robbins

Canuck and Other Stories edited by Rhea Côté Robbins
Brewer, Me. : Rheta Press, http://www.rhetapress.com/

Poetry included in: *French Connections: A Gathering of
Franco-American Poets*, published by Louisiana Litera-
ture Press.

Essays included in *Voyages A Maine Franco-American
and Acadian Reader*, published by Tillbury House.

Made in the USA
Monee, IL
24 June 2021